Complete Horoscope

Capricorn 2021

GW00542481

Monthly astrological forecasts for 2021

TATIANA BORSCH

Copyright © 2020 Tatiana Borsch.

All rights reserved. No part of this book may be reproduced, stored, or transmitted by any means—whether auditory, graphic, mechanical, or electronic—without written permission of the author, except in the case of brief excerpts used in critical articles and reviews. Unauthorized reproduction of any part of this work is illegal and is punishable by law.

Because of the dynamic nature of the Internet, any web addresses or links contained in this book may have changed since publication and may no longer be valid. The views expressed in this work are solely those of the author and do not necessarily reflect the views of the publisher, and the publisher hereby disclaims any responsibility for them.

This book is a work of non-fiction. Unless otherwise noted, the author and the publisher make no explicit guarantees as to the accuracy of the information contained in this book and in some cases, names of people and places have been altered to protect their privacy.

Any people depicted in stock imagery provided by Getty Images are models, and such images are being used for illustrative purposes only.

Certain stock imagery © Getty Images.

Contents

2021 - Birth of a new world

Based on the events of this year, my 2020 predictions, which were published on my website and in *SWAAY* magazine, are coming true (I write this article in summer 2020). We are bearing witness to an era of change; the world is teetering on the brink, and everything we thought was permanent and unshakable has turned out not to be. What else lies ahead?

It is impossible to separate the events of 2020 and 2021. These are years of major shifts, with an effect on each country, each home, and each individual. 2020's developments will continue in 2021, and there is simply no equivalent in modern history. It's safe to say that mankind has not experienced these kinds of changes in a very long time.

Major astrological events during this period are:

The first conjunction of Saturn and Jupiter in the air element will take place in Aquarius. This extremely significant event will literally take place as 2020 becomes 2021- on December 25, 2020.

This means the dawn of the Age of Aquarius, which almost everyone has heard about.

The Age of Aquarius is very long, lasting 2,160 years. It is determined by the Earth's shift from one axis to another. This transition period from one age to another can last a long time. Many astrologers believe that it will last at least 100 years. The last 20 years have been turbulent-they were vital preparation for the adoption of new rules for a new era.

All of this means that 2020 is the last year of the outgoing Age of Pisces, and 2021 is the first year of the Age of Aquarius.

Shifting eras is always linked with global shocks, crises of civilization, and economic and cultural revolutions, as well as a new perspective on religious teachings. Even the climate usually undergoes major changes.

Summer and autumn 2020, and all of 2021, are clear indicators of that.

The second most important astrological phenomenon is conflict between Saturn and Uranus, which will continue throughout 2021.

Saturn will square Uranus several times in 2021 – we can divide them into the following periods: January-March, May-the first half of July, December 2021-January 2022.

During these periods, we can expect many problems to rear their heads. It is hard to say exactly how this will influence each individual person as part of a general prediction – everything depends on your personal data, though, generally speaking, I can say that we will see the following trends in during these periods of 2021:

I.   First of all, we can expect the economic crisis to expand in scope. Many people will lose their jobs, and companies will go bankrupt.

II. In many countries, we will see social breakdown. People will organize strikes and demonstrations, and the overarching theme will be their discontent with authorities and the current order. We will see confrontation between society and power structures.

III. In global hotspots, we may see new deployments of military force or reescalation of conflict.

IV. For individuals, problems that began in 2019 or 2020 will continue, though this time, things may worsen. Remember – a chain is only as strong as its weakest link.

V.   The climate may undergo significant changes- flooding and forest fires will cause extensive damage. Large-scale migrations will be the result. In response, governments of countries in a better position may declare states of emergency or deploy troops in order to prevent unwanted migrants from crossing their borders.

VI. This interaction between Saturn and Uranus is indicative of conflict between old and new ways of life, and a difficult, irreconcilable struggle that will be reflected in all areas of life – social, economic, and political.

Saturn carries the energy of restrictions and structure. At the same time, Uranus is the planet of unexpected, revolutionary change (as well as high tech). Conflict between the two planets leads to sharp changes in existing reality. Transitioning to a new world and a new set of rules will lead to conflict.

Interaction between Saturn and Uranus speaks to opposition to both new and old ways of living, and of the rigid, irreconcilable struggle that is reflected in every sphere of life – social, economic, and political. Most peoples' lives will undergo dramatic changes, and they will have to adapt.

Economics and Politics

Saturn will square Uranus throughout 2021, and this will raise difficult questions – it is time for out with the old, in with the new. But replacing an old system with a new one is rarely a peaceful process. That is why the struggle between old and new economic orders will be a feature of 2020 and 2021.

Former economic systems will begin to transform, right before our very eyes, and these processes will go hand in hand with trade wars, political reckoning, and in some cases, armed conflict.

As the global financial crisis further unfolds, we can expect to see a stronger China, and weakened United States. Countries in the Western financial system will suffer greatly, particularly those in the Eurozone, and American political and economic satellites.

From an astrological perspective, the American presidential elections will take place during one of the most challenging periods of 2020. By now, we are used to political scandals every four years when they occur. However, I fear that the 2020 elections will put all others to shame when it comes to political upheaval.

On Election Day and the period leading up to it, Mercury and Mars will be in retrograde, which means that there will be significant incorrect or intentionally twisted information, crowds of protesters, and this will peak the last week before the elections take place, on November 3. Retrograde planets also point toward the opposition party trying to protest the election results, which will translate into large-scale scandal.

Donald Trump may be re-elected for a second term, if Joe Biden is his only opponent. Incriminating information on Biden will come to light in late September or October 2020, when he will simultaneously battle serious health issues. Generally speaking, Biden's horoscope is much weaker than Trump's.

Whoever ends up as President of the United States will have to face a series of problems in 2021- most of all conflict among members of his inner circle.

The horoscope of the United States, which was founded on the day of its Declaration of Independence, on July 04, 1776, in Philadelphia, Pennsylvania, USA, predicts that America's economic and political might will waste away, and this may take place more quickly than we can imagine.

This crisis in the American system will lead to a drop and depreciation in the US dollar in late 2020 or the first quarter of 2021. The US chart suggests that in 2021, the dollar will be replaced as a reserve currency.

As America weakens, it will face growing confrontations with other countries. In 2021, the US will wield less influence on political and economic allies.

There may even be tides of separatism within the States themselves. Even so, I do not think the United States is threatened by the same fate as the USSR – it is unlikely to disintegrate. But it is possible that in late 2020 or early 2021, some states will declare their desire to secede, and even take some decisive steps in that direction, but full secession is not in the cards. Nonetheless, the struggle will be very difficult for America's political elite and society as a whole.

Large-scale social protests and unrest, which we saw in 2019 and 2020 will continue in 2021, though they may become more aggressive in nature.

This does not only apply to the United States. Social activism will grow worldwide. Mottos of the Age of Aquarius are FREEDOM, EQUALITY, and BROTHERHOOD, and they will be brandished in many countries around the world. This time, the conflict will not only be over ethnic or racial issues, but also pit social classes against each other – the rich versus the poor.

During the second half of 2020, and nearly all of 2021, expect an economic crisis that will spare nearly no country around the world. Many will blame their current governments, and brutal confrontations between citizens and the authorities will follow, oppositions will become active, demonstrations will take place, and instability in some countries may go so far as to topple current regimes.

England will also be dragged into financial crisis, and according to its horoscope, the worst period countrywide is likely to begin in December 2020, and last until September 2023. Expect financial problems, changes in the Royal Family (the Queen is likely to leave the throne between December 2020 and July 2021), and also innovative changes to how the country is governed.

There are also indications that in the summer and fall of 2020, a financial crisis is likely in the Russian Federation, and it will continue into 2021.

During this period, President Putin's horoscope contains indications of a systemic crisis, financial shortages, and growing opposition movements. Any leader's horoscope is largely a reflection of the state of his or her country.

Money

All countries will lean more strongly toward virtual currencies and cryptocurrencies, which will be accepted by many countries' governments over the next three to five years. This will make it easier to control cash flow, and with it, all of us.

Our reality will increasingly take place virtually, and professionals in this arena will make up the most sought-after and highly-paid class of workers.

As far as personal finance, the Zodiac sign horoscopes included in my book, "Complete Horoscope 2021" offer more specific information. But generally speaking, during a transition period, it is better to refrain from taking risks, and best to avoid investing your money in get-rich-quick schemes.

What's more, there is a saying "Don't risk your house on a sure thing"-now, that is surprisingly relevant.

Personal life

A crisis is a crisis, but love is an eternal concept. So long as humans exist, they will live and love. 2021 will likely also be a year of major changes in this arena. While tragedy will befall some, others will find happiness.

Unstable partnerships are likely to fall apart, and all the problems faced by unhappy couples are likely to rear their ugly heads.

Unexpected breakups are a possibility, and in many cases, this will be related to an existential crisis, internal discomfort, or maybe even material losses.

Couples with a sincere bond and real affection for one another may be able to take their relationship to the next level, for example, they may begin living together, or get married.

The political, economic, and social shifts underway might force many to move, find a new place to live, or acquire real estate. Many people may also find themselves immersed in issues related to housing- buying or restoring a home, and in some cases, that may be related to moving to another city or even abroad.

In that scenario, be careful and pay attention- due to the conflict between Saturn and Uranus, it is not worth making any investments in a completed construction or second home unless the project has already been proven.

People will begin to seriously reconsider their views on the concept of marriage in the near future. During the Age of Aquarius, bonds between people will be built on ideas of equality and spiritual unity.

The current trend of increasing numbers of non-traditional relationships will only grow stronger.

Differences between the sexes will gradually fade away, as Aquarius is the sign of unisex. Marriage itself will begin to resemble the classic model less and less, as it becomes free, and in some cases, "open". This may bring both advantages and serious disadvantages. Obviously, freedom is a good thing. But that freedom often goes hand in hand with loneliness.

Conflict between Saturn and Uranus will lead to a generational conflict. Saturn represents the older generation, parents, while Uranus represents rebellious children. That means that the younger generation will actively push back against pressure from their elders, and the older generation will need to become wiser and more flexible.

Health

Technology will play a greater role in medicine, affecting every branch of it.

The union of Saturn and Jupiter, and their tension toward Uranus suggest unexpected deaths, which may be due to various types of accidents and cataclysms.

Those suffering from chronic cardiovascular or spinal diseases should take special precautions.

We may encounter a "second wave" of coronavirus, or outbreaks of new, unknown diseases.

I entitled this article "Birth of a New World". Birth is a painful process, and a mother's body undergoes significant changes, but the fact remains that birth is a great joy for parents and loved ones. The same can be said for 2021. It will not be an easy year, and many will have a difficult time – whether they face problems at work or in their personal life, but that is the logical continuation of the period we live in. We will gain experience and knowledge, and see the emergence of new technology, which will open a new chapter in human history. I am certain that after a transition period, the Age of Aquarius will be the beginning of a new, wonderful world.

Tatiana Borsch

July 12, 2020

2021 Overview for Capricorn

The last few years have been a bit of a rush for you at work. You did a lot, but as one chapter comes to a close, another one opens. As before, your protector Saturn is guiding you both forward and upward.

Work. Major changes are not predicted at work, and revolution is not on the horizon. However, Jupiter is shifting to the sector of the sky responsible for moves, changes, and you're suddenly feeling like you can't sit still.

Slowly but surely, entrepreneurs are seeing their plans come to fruition, and this is related to growing your business in faraway places. For now, though, they are just plans, and translating them into action won't be possible until 2022.

The most persistent Capricorns will begin negotiations on this in late May, June, and July, as well as December.

Employees will also strengthen their position at work. Things keep moving ahead, and your money is growing.

Money. Despite the obvious benefits at work, and a higher income, you can't say things are totally calm when it comes to the material area of your life. It isn't necessarily due to a lack of income, but growing demands from your loved ones, especially children.

Love and family. Your personal life is not particularly stable in 2021. Even happily married Capricorns might argue frequently and annoy each other more often.

Problems with children will complete the picture. Maybe they will be rebellious, misbehave, stage a real mutiny. While in some cases, this is a natural part of growing up, that is unlikely to be true most of the time. Throughout 2021, you'll find yourself spending a hefty amount of money on your children's needs, and the stars strongly urge you to separate actual needs from capriciousness - but only you can make that happen.

For most Capricorns in a relationship, 2021 will be a real test of strength. Uranus - the planet of surprises and the unexpected - is holding firmly to the love sector of your sky, and this time, the surprises may not be so pleasant.

Perhaps your partner will act out in ways you didn't expect, that is, making moral or material complaints. On the other hand, you yourself may be making a decision to develop the relationship, and this will be a difficult step in every direction.

Health. In 2021, your energy is rather low, and you may be experiencing mood swings, linked to the various facets of your life colliding. The stars recommend that you live a healthy lifestyle all year long, and learn to take a step back and look at problems from above. That will keep you strong in body and spirit.

You may have to take care of a family member's health in the coming year, which you will do, sparing no effort.

January

"Flexibility" is the word of the month. Think of workarounds. Attempts to get ahead will only lead to negative results, and that goes for both work and love.

Work. This month, you may not be up to working, and most likely all of your thoughts will be wrapped up in your personal life. That will be the case for everyone in the first half of January.

You will get busy at work during the second half of January, but several different issues that have been marinating for some time now may prevent you from going full speed ahead. You may find yourself disagreeing with a friend, like-minded individuals, or a superior, and, as usual, it's about money. If you are facing a similar situation, remember that it is not going away any time soon.

Your relationships with colleagues in other cities or abroad are, however, going well, and in the first half of the month you may go on a successful trip.

Money. Financially, January is not particularly promising, as you have a lot of expenses and most of them are related to your personal life. You may face financial problems involving your children, or your partner's demands.

Love and family. Many Capricorns will be immersed in personal problems this month.

Children will cause a lot of headaches for those with families; things may get out of control, and getting things back on track may take up an outsize portion of the family budget. This may go along with conflicts and emotional tests. It is likely that all this will be unexpected, but in fact, it has been a long time coming. So, collect yourself and come up with a plan of action- there is no other way out.

January is a difficult month for those in relationships. Turbulent relationships may become serious, and more than simply feelings are at play – it will revolve around money or other things of material value.

Otherwise, a loved one will need a large amount of money from you as support, and if you agree to it, it is likely that you will avoid drama. However, these problems are unlikely to end in January, they will continue next month, when things will only get worse.

Health. During the first half of the month, you are feeling energetic and in good health. But during the second half of the month, your well-being takes a turn for the worse, and things may get out of control- you are certainly not used to this. Don't let this get you down! There is always a silver lining, setbacks can teach us a lot.

February

It's best you come up with a well-thought-out and detailed plan of action this month, as it is bound to be difficult and full of conflict. This is the only thing that can save you from disaster, whether at work or at home.

Work. This month, be sure to double-check any information, and don't take anyone at their word. Otherwise, you run the risk of being dragged into various problems- most of all, financial issues, which, in February, will come to a head.

Entrepreneurs and managers will have to settle some real estate, as well as various services. These bills may be higher than you expected. From February 7 to 20, many Capricorns will likely face losses, so take any steps possible to shield yourself, and don't rush things. Take the time to carefully check each account before signing anything and making a final decision.

Money. As stated above, February is a disastrous month, and this may be due to work, or possibly your personal, romantic, or family life.

Love and family. Many Capricorns will see major developments in their personal relationships.

Families will experience continuing problems involving their children. In many cases, children will behave inappropriately, which will lead to conflicts and huge expenses. Keep a very close eye on this sensitive facet of your life, as the problems are unlikely to end this month, and will instead continue into the future.

Alternatively, you will have to help your youngest family members, and that help is likely to be material in nature.

A real storm bodes for couples this month, and if the relationship was already hanging by a thread, February is the month that thread may finally snap. However, after arguments and separation, you may reconcile, which has happened before.

Health. Most of the month, you are feeling somewhat sluggish, and February's unstable atmosphere may drive you to a serious nervous breakdown. Remember, doctors agree that your nervous system is the cause of all ailments. So, try to remain calm, keep a cool head, and remember the wise words of Solomon – "This too, shall pass".

March

March will bring you a series of surprises, and this time, they will be appreciated. The heavens are starting to shine down on you.

Work. You're on a lucky streak at work. You have renewed ties with colleagues from other cities or abroad, and can expect a successful trip. This is the perfect time to work on your relationship with colleagues and subordinates, as well as management.

If you want to change something at work or look for a new job, now is the best time to do it. As they say, knock down every door, and someone is bound to open!

What's more, March is an ideal time for studying, creative activities, for example, touring new cities and countries.

Money. Throughout March, the financial landscape looks sustainable. You are earning more money, and expect to receive the largest amounts on March 1, 2, 9, 10, 20, 21, 28, and 29.

Expenses are less than they were in previous months, but right now they are related to your personal life- someone close to you or your children.

Love and family. You still have problems in your personal life, but this time, they don't seem insurmountable. Your children are better behaved, and their problems are easier to deal with. Couples' relationships are also calmer and more even, and if you are still together following a recent argument, then this is a good sign for the future.

If you have already separated, you are willing to take a step toward reconciliation. There is still hope of continuing the relationship.

Health. In March, you are feeling energetic and have no reason to fear illness.

April

You are an excellent manager, and this month, your organizational skills will be on full display, both at work and at home.

Work. April is a busy time for you at work, and your biggest task will be the issue of major changes that will affect every area of your work.

Entrepreneurs and managers might think of a way to expand your business, and in some cases, that will lead to restructuring existing facilities, and in others, acquiring new ones. In either case, things will run smoothly and without a hitch.

Managers are able to count on knowledgeable, detailed, and responsible assistants and subordinates. Employees might be fully immersed in family affairs, but work won't wait! That is why many Capricorns will have to constantly juggle both work and family responsibilities.

Money. Financially, April is a successful month for you. Money will be coming in regularly, and you now have significantly more of it. In addition to your usual sources of income, this month, you can count on additional profit from various real estate transactions. Expect to receive the largest sums of money on April 6, 7, 15-17, 25, and 26.

Love and family. Your personal life is settling down, though you can't say it's exactly quiet. Many families will be experiencing problems with their children, and this may involve some expenses. But this time, these problems don't look quite so serious. The worst may be over, and things should get much easier from now on.

Many families are dealing with home improvement and day-to-day issues right now. That may be repairs, acquiring various household items, or decorating.

You may acquire some real estate, and in many cases, that will involve your children.

April is also a good month for couples. The challenges over the last several months are resolved, and you might go on a trip, which will smooth over any remaining conflict.

Health. This month, you are not feeling particularly energetic, so find some time to relax and spend time in nature. You will have a change.

May

Your family and personal relationships might become more important to you as the spring colors bloom. But remember to give yourself some breathing room, your work will still be here tomorrow!

Work. The first ten days of the month are not particularly promising for work and financial transactions. The best thing you can do is deepen your relationship with colleagues in other cities or abroad, or even travel to meet them.

The second half of the month, you are busier and things are looking more positive, you might start thinking about ideas that for one reason or another were set aside, and the details on how to make them come to life. During this period, managers will strongly be able to count on their subordinates, and employees on their colleagues.

You will also see some major changes underway when it comes to work. Many will have plans to launch their business in another city or abroad, and eventually, these ideas will become reality. You will have to make a lot of changes though, for that to happen- the way you see things, get ready for the coming changes might be your theme for the second half of May.

Money. Your money situation is up and down, all month. A lot of your income will arrive between May 11 and 31, and expect to receive the largest sums on May 4, 12, 13, 22-24, 30, and 31.

You will have expenses during the first half of the month, and they will not be minor. Most of them will once again be related to your children or loved ones.

Love and family. Your personal life is also shifting. Parents are still worried about their children's futures and continuing to invest large amounts of money in their education and well-being. You are in this for the long haul, so get ready to open your wallet at any moment.

Many families are starting to discuss a move, and in some cases, these plans involve another city or country. Everyone will implement their plans differently, but things are unlikely to remain as they are now.

Your relationship with relatives is suddenly much more dynamic, and one of your close relatives might come visit you or, alternatively, you might see them where they live. In the case of couples on the rocks, things will get more complicated, and you can expect yet more conflict during the second half of the month.

The first half of May is difficult for couples in love, when for various reasons, they may see less of each other than they would have liked.

Health. This month, you are feeling good and don't expect any illnesses. During the second half of the month, however, be careful while traveling or driving. The likelihood of accidents during this period is rather high.

June

Take a closer look around, especially at those closest to you. Take steps to protect yourself!

Work. This month, you might get carried away with new ideas and projects. It would be good for you to make sure that they are feasible, as you may confuse your fantasy with reality.

Many Capricorns might have plans involving faraway places and foreign countries, and during various periods of 2021, you will be taking your first steps toward making them a reality.

For now, though, you are in the planning stage, and can expect a lot of bumps in the road ahead. You will encounter some of them this month, and some a little later on. But you're tough, and not used to losing. So once again, you will overcome the obstacles and play by your own rules.

In any case, the stars strongly encourage managers and entrepreneurs to keep a close eye on subordinates, as trouble is brewing within the ranks, over the coming changes. You may also be dealing with red tape, a lack of people you need, and a lot of needless fussing around.

Employees should do their jobs carefully and be cautious when communicating with their colleagues. You might also be a victim of untrustworthy information, or pulled into unflattering intrigue.

Money. Your financial situation is up and down. On one hand, money might be coming in as usual, predictably. But expenses will unexpectedly rise. Most of the time, this is related to your personal life and your children's and loved one's needs. Expect to spend the most in mid- and late June.

Love and family. Your personal life is not stable, right now. Many families are once again dealing with a problem involving their children. Again, most of your budget is going toward the younger generation's needs, and it may happen more than once.

Couples can expect stormy skies, as well. Some relationships have simply run their course and will end this month. Whether the separation is permanent or temporary depends on you. Maybe you want to have the last word, and it will be harsh – but you will come to regret this, so don't burn any bridges right now. There is always time for that later.

Many Capricorns are clearly dealing with the prospect of moving, and this will become a reality a little later, in 2022.

Health. This month, you are not particularly energetic, so take care of yourself and be vigilant. Also, be careful while traveling and driving.

July

July looks like a rehearsal before your big premiere. Everything that starts right now will take you down a positive path in the future.

Work. You are undergoing major changes at work. Many Capricorns are thinking about opening their own business in another city or abroad and taking steps in that direction. For now, you're in the planning stage, once you start moving toward your goal, things will come to fruition. You might take a trip, but you won't know how things will turn out until you're already there.

In all cases, you can expect your business partners, who have shown themselves to be responsible and reliable, to lend a helping hand.

Entrepreneurs and managers should keep a close eye on all documentation and paperwork, and also monitor their subordinates, as any errors on their part may throw a wrench in all of your plans.

Money. Financially speaking, this month might be a disaster. You will be bleeding money, and in some cases, your expenses may be related to business development, while in others, you can blame your personal life, likely either your family or children.

Love and family. Your personal life will continue to see the same problems you had in the past. Many families will be resolving matters related to their children, and the price tag will not be cheap. Take a look at every option, you likely know the root of your problems, and that is the most important thing if you are going to resolve things.

Throughout this, you can count on help from your spouse or someone close to you. Seeking common ground with your children will lighten their load.

If you are expecting changes with your children, someone close to you will provide assistance.

Many families are considering a move, and slowly starting to make plans in that direction.

Couples' relationships are feeling the pressure from the stars, and only those who truly live for love will go the distance.

For all relationships, the first ten days of July will be the most difficult period, when you can expect conflict to break out. During the rest of the month, things will quiet down significantly, though that is not exactly sustainable. Most likely, you will have to grapple with some problems and mitigate them, somehow.

Health. In July, your energy levels are not their highest, and those suffering from chronic heart or spinal conditions should be especially careful, as well as those with weakened immune systems for any reason.

August

Traditionally, August is not the best time of the year for you. The situations you will encounter this month will strongly remind you of everything you went through in the recent past. That will help you cope, and possibly even resolve your task.

Work. During the first ten days of August, you will start actively expanding your business, and, most likely, that will take place in another city or abroad. You may have plans related to setting up another business for this purpose.

Your relationship with colleagues out of town or abroad is moving along very well, and this will become most apparent between August 11 and 20, as well as all of September. You might take a trip, which will be highly successful, especially if you have a detailed plan in hand, and a well-developed project.

Money. Financially, the first ten days of August will be the most difficult. During this time, for various reasons, you will end up spending large amounts of money. In some cases, the expenses may be related to business development, while in others, they will stem from your family's needs, particularly those of your children.

Love and family. Your personal life is looking tumultuous and stressful during the first ten days of the month. Once again, parents will have to deal with problems involving their children, which will lead to major expenses. In some cases, you will have to make painful decisions related to your children's affairs, and in others, you will simply have to put up the funds for their education, training, and development.

This is also a difficult time for couples. You may have unexpected arguments, for various reasons, or end up spending some time apart. During the second half of the month, however, you will reach a compromise, and it is very likely that you will go on a trip. The second half of the month, as well as all of September, is a great time for you to get clarity on both personal and professional matters, while significantly improving them, as well.

Health. You are not particularly energetic in August, and many Capricorns might not feel particularly confident or cheerful. Those who are elderly or weak should be particularly vigilant, as should those suffering from chronic heart or spinal disease. The last ten days of the month are looking much calmer, as the stars will be on your side for everything, including your health.

September

Sometimes, there comes a time when you need to make serious changes in certain areas of your life. September is one of those times. Onward!

Work. This month, you are unlikely to spend much time sitting at home – you have travel, meetings, and business to take care of, and that is your theme, all month long.

Entrepreneurs will link their plans to colleagues from far away, and spare no efforts in reaching their cherished goals.

It is possible that all the movement in September will be preliminary in nature, and the main events are for later on. They will focus on developing your business in another city or abroad. In many cases, September's agreements will be directly related to these planned changes.

During the first twenty days of the month, you are on a quite favorable streak, which applies to all Capricorns, regardless of where they work. Employees will strengthen their position at work this month, or receive new, attractive offers.

Entrepreneurs can count on unexpected deals and profits from previous work.

During the last ten days of the month, things will be less exciting, and that will be noticeable closer to the end of the month. For that reason, you should try to schedule major events and meetings for the first twenty days of September.

Money. Financially speaking, this month is not bad at all. You will be receiving money regularly, and slightly more of it, too. You can expect to receive the largest sums of money on September 8-19, 17-18, 26, and 28. Your expenses are minimal, and in any case, they are often for pleasure, rather than necessity.

Love and family. Your personal life is also going through positive changes. Situations involving children will improve greatly, and you will have to find a common ground with them this month. In some cases, you will find a shared cause, and in others, you will find a way to relax or otherwise spend time having fun together It seems that the stars will stop testing your strength in this very important area of your life.

Spouses will not be particularly joyful this month, but you also won't find sadness. Things might be best for unmarried couples – you might find your feelings are suddenly much stronger; even if you recently separated due to an argument, you will be able to find a path to each other's hearts. You might go on a trip together, which will help strengthen the relationship.

Single people and those who have been disappointed by past partners are in for a real surprise – an unexpected meeting, a lively romance, which will add some excitement to your life, even if it does not last for long.

Health. Many Capricorns will get a surge of energy, another gift during what will be a wonderful month.

October

In October, you will try to change the world, or at least your surroundings. And in much of this, you will succeed.

Work. This month, you are up to your neck in work. Change is on the horizon, and your main task in October is to be prepared for them. In order to do that, you should carry out a careful analysis of your business, and then implement any necessary adjustments.

You will make some decisions this month, and some later on, but as an excellent strategist, you are able to imagine the future, and might start taking your first steps in that direction.

Most likely, this will involve expanding your business, and in many cases, that will take place in another city or abroad. Though the biggest changes will not be until 2022, nothing is preventing you from laying the groundwork already. Your friends might be intermediaries between you and future colleagues.

Employees might see changes in leadership at their place of employment, though these changes are only to your benefit. In October, you might discuss a promotion at work, or significantly expanding your authority.

Money. Your financial outlook is stable, you are earning more, and spending less. You can expect to receive the largest sums of money on October 6, 7, 14, 15, 23-25, and 28.

Love and family. Your personal life is not your priority in October, but this is a good thing. Parents will be less worried about their children, and problems are gradually resolving themselves. There is also hope that this positive process will continue in the future.

It is hard to predict the outlook for couples, but if you are already together, then that's already a good thing. Is there hope for a happy ending? Of course, there is! Let your relationship develop in its own way, and don't be afraid to take the first step.

Health. In October, you are healthy, attentive, and energetic. In a word, you feel ready to move mountains. Your enthusiasm is so contagious, though, that you won't have to – the mountains will move themselves.

November

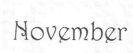

This month, you might expect the unexpected – your emotions will prevail over logic, when you should strive for the opposite, which is the only way to exert any control over events in your personal and professional life.

Work. Just like last month, your career and work are your priorities this month. But right now, your goal is to strengthen your relationship with friends and influential members of society. That will not be an easy task, as in exchange for certain services, you may have to fulfill various demands. Most likely, that means money or other things of material value. But if you are ready for that kind of development, there is no way around it.

With the exception of this issue, work is still going well; your ties to colleagues from other cities or abroad are growing, and you may even go on a successful trip.

Many Capricorns are laying the groundwork for opening their own business in another city or abroad, and in 2022, that will become a reality.

Money. As far as finances are concerned, November might be bumpy. You might face major expenses all month long, and most of them will come during the first half of the month. In some cases, this may involve money paid to resolve work-related problems, and in others, it will be due to a difficult situation with your family, possibly your children's affairs.

Love and family. During the first twenty days of the month, you might have to deal with difficult situations, as well as delicate, sensitive matters.

Parents will have to deal with many problems involving their children, which will once again lead to emotional outbursts and unexpected expenses. You are aware of the problem, but this time, it may take a new, unpleasant turn for the entire family. During the second half of the month, things will improve, thanks to your good faith and effort. The problem may continue to cause you stress for some time, and the stars recommend that you carefully study the entire situation and its root cause. This is necessary, if you don't want things to repeat themselves later on.

For couples, November is also a challenging time. You can expect sudden conflicts from the very beginning of the month, and things will clear up a little later. You will see that there was, in fact, no major problem, and you will understand everything and forgive a lot. What's more, you are looking at the issue from a very close range. So, don't stick to hard and fast rules, take the first step, and you will be pleasantly surprised with your partner's reaction.

Health. This month, you are healthy, energetic, and attractive – and everyone fate sends your way is taking note.

December

The last month, you have been working on a difficult task in unfamiliar waters. The past and future are strangely intertwined, and you need to say goodbye to the former and accept the latter.

Work. December is a time of transition from a period of high anxiety in the past, to an unusual and very positive future.

Your problems from the past include a challenging relationship with an adversary. Once again, you will have to deal with grievances, which are most likely financial in nature. You might also face audits or even legal problems.

Along with that, entrepreneurs will once again have an idea for expanding their business, but this time, in another city or abroad. In order to reach that goal, you must take advantage of all of your contacts. If you do, you won't have to wait long to see results. Though you are only in the negotiation phase, these are the first steps in the right direction, and there is no doubt that 2022 is the year you will make things happen.

Changes at work will also affect employees, most all when it comes to changes in the organizational structure of your workplace, which may spark various types of intrigue and competition.

Money. Your financial situation is contradictory. On one hand, you will not find yourself without any money at all. On the other, though, your expenses will be very high in December. This may be related to your issues at work, as well as your family and personal relationships.

Love and family. Your personal life may once again be full of problems from previous months. You will do everything in order to help your children, and a lot of your efforts will pay off. But they will need money once again, and you will have to give it to them. There is hope that in the near future, this issue will be entirely behind you, and next year, it shouldn't stress you, anymore.

Many Capricorns are on the brink of major changes – your plans may be related to a move, which might play out in 2022. You may move in town, to a home in the country, or possibly abroad.

Couples might find themselves arguing frequently and periodically wondering if they should break things off. But if your love is still alive, it will have the last say, over your rigidity, stinginess, pride, and ambitions. That is the way it should be, anyway!

Health. This month, you are not very energetic, and that will be most notable during the new moon and eclipse – December 4 and 5. Be careful and take it easy for a few days. The work will still be there tomorrow. During the first half of December, that is particularly relevant advice.

A guide to Zodiac compatibility

Often, when we meet a person, we get a feeling that they are good and we take an instant liking to them. Another person, however, gives us immediate feelings of distrust, fear and hostility. Is there an astrological reason why people say that 'the first impression is the most accurate'? How can we detect those who will bring us nothing but trouble and unhappiness?

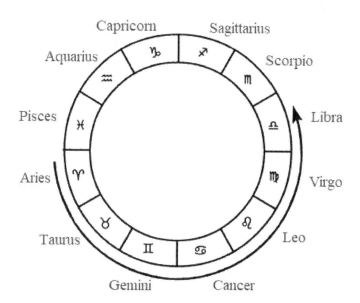

Without going too deeply into astrological subtleties unfamiliar to some readers, it is possible to determine the traits according to which friendship, love or business relationships will develop.

Let's begin with problematic relationships - our most difficult are with our **8th sign**. For example, for Aries the 8th sign is Scorpio, for Taurus it is Sagittarius and so on. Finding your 8th sign is easy; assume your own sign to be first (see above Figure) and then move eight signs counter clockwise around the Zodiac circle. This is also how the other signs (fourth, ninth and so on) that we mention are to be found.

Ancient astrologers variously referred to the 8th sign as the symbol of death, of destruction, of fated love or unfathomable attraction. In astrological terms, this pair is called 'master and slave' or 'boa constrictor and rabbit', with the role of 'master' or 'boa constrictor' being played by our 8th sign.

This relationship is especially difficult for politicians and business people.

We can take the example of a recent political confrontation in the USA. Hilary Clinton is a Scorpio while Donald Trump is a Gemini - her 8th sign. Even though many were certain that Clinton would be elected President, she lost.

To take another example, Hitler was a Taurus and his opponents – Stalin and Churchill - were both of his 8th sign, Sagittarius. The result of their confrontation is well known. Interestingly, the Russian Marshals who dealt crushing military blows to Hitler and so helped end the Third Reich - Konstantin Rokossovsky and Georgy Zhukov - were also Sagittarian, Hitler's 8th sign.

In another historical illustration, Lenin was also a Taurus. Stalin was of Lenin's 8th sign and was ultimately responsible for the downfall and possibly death of his one-time comrade-in-arms.

Business ties with those of our 8th sign are hazardous as they ultimately lead to stress and loss; both financial and moral. So, do not tangle with your 8th sign and never fight with it - your chances of winning are remote!

Such relationships are very interesting in terms of love and romance, however. We are magnetically attracted to our 8th sign and even though it may be very intense physically, it is very difficult for family life;

'Feeling bad when together, feeling worse when apart'.

As an example, let us take the famous lovers - George Sand who was Cancer and Alfred de Musset who was Sagittarius. Cancer is the 8th sign for Sagittarius, and the story of their crazy two-year love affair was the subject of much attention throughout France. Critics and writers were divided into 'Mussulist' and 'Sandist' camps; they debated fiercely about who was to blame for the sad ending to their love story - him or her. It's hard to imagine the energy needed to captivate the public for so long, but that energy was destructive for the couple. Passion raged in their hearts, but neither of them was able to comprehend their situation.

Georges Sand wrote to Musset, "*I ₁on't love you anymore, an₁ I will always a₁ore you. I ₁on't want you anymore, an₁ I can't ₁o without you. It seems that nothing but a heavenly lightning strike can heal me by ₁estroying me. Goo₁-bye! Stay or go, but ₁on't say that I am not suffering. This is the only thing that can make me suffer even more, my love, my life, my bloo₁! Go away, but kill me, leaving.*" Musset replied only in brief, but its power surpassed Sand's tirade, "*When you embrace₁ me, I felt something that is still bothering me, making it impossible for me to approach another woman.*" These two people loved each other passionately and for two years lived together in a powder keg of passion, hatred and treachery.

When someone enters into a romantic liaison with their 8th sign, there will be no peace; indeed, these relationships are very attractive to those who enjoy the edgy, the borderline and, in the Dostoevsky style, the melodramatic. The first to lose interest in the relationship is, as a rule, the 8th sign.

If, by turn of fate, our child is born under our 8th sign, they will be very different from us and, in some ways, not live up to our expectations. It may be best to let them choose their own path.

In business and political relationships, the combination with our **12th sign** is also a complicated one.

We can take two political examples. Angela Merkel is a Cancer while Donald Trump is a Gemini - her 12th sign. This is why their relations are strained and complicated and we can even perhaps assume that the American president will achieve his political goals at her expense. Boris Yeltsin (Aquarius) was the 12th sign to Mikhail Gorbachev (Pisces) and it was Yeltsin who managed to dethrone the champion of Perestroika.

Even ancient astrologers noticed that our relationships with our 12th signs can never develop evenly; it is one of the most curious and problematic combinations. They are our hidden enemies and they seem to be digging a hole for us; they ingratiate themselves with us, discover our innermost secrets. As a result, we become bewildered and make mistakes when we deal with them. Among the Roman emperors murdered by members of their entourage, there was an interesting pattern - all the murderers were the 12th sign of the murdered.

We can also see this pernicious effect in Russian history: the German princess Alexandra (Gemini) married the last Russian Tsar Nicholas II (Taurus) - he was her 12th sign and brought her a tragic death. The wicked genius Grigory Rasputin (Cancer) made friends with Tsarina Alexandra, who was his 12th sign, and was murdered as a result of their odd friendship. The weakness of Nicholas II was exposed, and his authority reduced after the death of the economic and social reformer Pyotr Stolypin, who was his 12th sign. Thus, we see a chain of people whose downfall was brought about by their 12th sign.

So, it makes sense to be cautious of your 12th sign, especially if you have business ties. Usually, these people know much more about us than we want them to and they will often reveal our secrets for personal gain if it suits them. However, the outset of these relationships is, as a rule, quite normal - sometimes the two people will be friends, but sooner or later one will betray the other one or divulge a secret; inadvertently or not.

In terms of romantic relationships, our 12th sign is gentle, they take care of us and are tender towards us. They know our weaknesses well but accept them with understanding. It is they who guide us, although sometimes almost imperceptibly. Sexual attraction is usually strong.

For example, Meghan Markle is a Leo, the 12th sign for Prince Harry, who is a Virgo. Despite Queen Elizabeth II being lukewarm about the match, Harry's love was so strong that they did marry.

If a child is our 12th sign, it later becomes clear that they know all our secrets, even those that they are not supposed to know. It is very difficult to control them as they do everything in their own way.

Relations with our 7th **sign** are also interesting. They are like our opposite; they have something to learn from us while we, in turn, have something to learn from them. This combination, in business and personal relationships, can be very positive and stimulating provided that both partners are quite intelligent and have high moral standards but if not, constant misunderstandings and challenges follow. Marriage or co-operation with the 7th sign can only exist as the union of two fully-fledged individuals and in this case love, significant business achievements and social success are possible.

However, the combination can be not only interesting, but also quite complicated.

An example is Angelina Jolie, a Gemini, and Brad Pitt, a Sagittarius. This is a typical bond with a 7th sign - it's lively and interesting, but rather stressful. Although such a couple may quarrel and even part from time to time, never do they lose interest in each other.

This may be why this combination is more stable in middle-age when there is an understanding of the true nature of marriage and partnership. In global, political terms, this suggests a state of eternal tension - a cold war - for example between Yeltsin (Aquarius) and Bill Clinton (Leo).

Relations with our 9th **sign** are very good; they are our teacher and advisor - one who reveals things we are unaware of and our relationships with them very often involve travel or re-location. The combination can lead to spiritual growth and can be beneficial in terms of business.

Although, for example, Trump and Putin are political opponents, they can come to an understanding and even feel a certain sympathy for each other because Putin is a Libra while Trump is a Gemini, his 9th sign.

This union is also quite harmonious for conjugal and romantic relationships.

We treat our **3rd sign** somewhat condescendingly. They are like our younger siblings; we teach them and expect them to listen attentively. Our younger brothers and sisters are more often than not born under this sign. In terms of personal and sexual relationships, the union is not very inspiring and can end quickly, although this is not always the case. In terms of business, it is fairly average as it often connects partners from different cities or countries.

We treat our **5th sign** as a child and we must take care of them accordingly. The combination is not very good for business, however, since our 5th sign triumphs over us in terms of connections and finances, and thereby gives us very little in return save for love or sympathy. However, they are very good for family and romantic relationships, especially if the 5th sign is female. If a child is born as a 5th sign to their parents, their relationship will be a mutually smooth, loving and understanding one that lasts a lifetime.

Our **10th sign** is a born leader. Depending on the spiritual level of those involved, both pleasant and tense relations are possible; the relationship is often mutually beneficial in the good times but mutually disruptive in the bad times. In family relations, our 10th sign always tries to lead and will do so according to their intelligence and upbringing.

Our **4th sign** protects our home and can act as a sponsor to strengthen our financial or moral positions. Their advice should be heeded in all cases as it can be very effective, albeit very unobtrusive. If a woman takes this role, the relationship can be long and romantic, since all the spouse's wishes are usually met one way or another. Sometimes, such couples achieve great social success; for instance, Hilary Clinton, a Scorpio is the 4th sign to Bill Clinton, a Leo. On the other hand, if the husband is the 4th sign for his wife, he tends to be henpecked. There is often a strong sexual attraction. Our 4th sign can improve our living conditions and care for us in a parental way. If a child is our 4th sign, they are close to us and support us affectionately.

Relations with our **11th sign** are often either friendly or patronizing; we treat them reverently, while they treat us with friendly condescension. Sometimes, these relationships develop in an 'older brother' or 'high-ranking friend' sense; indeed, older brothers and sisters are often our 11th sign. In terms of personal and sexual relationships, our 11th sign is always inclined to enslave us. This tendency is most clearly manifested in such alliances as Capricorn and Pisces or Leo and Libra. A child who is the 11th sign to their parents will achieve greater success than their parents, but this will only make the parents proud.

Our **2nd sign** should bring us financial or other benefits; we receive a lot from them in both our business and our family life. In married couples, the 2nd sign usually looks after the financial situation for the benefit of the family. Sexual attraction is strong.

Our **6th sign** is our 'slave'; we always benefit from working with them and it's very difficult for them to escape our influence. In the event of hostility, especially if they have provoked the conflict, they receive a powerful retaliatory strike. In personal relations, we can almost destroy them by making them dance to our tune. For example, if a husband doesn't allow his wife to work or there are other adverse family circumstances, she gradually becomes lost as an individual despite being surrounded by care. This is the best-case scenario; worse outcomes are possible. Our 6th sign has a strong sexual attraction to us because we are the fatal 8th sign for them; we cool down quickly, however, and often make all kinds of demands. If the relationship with our 6th sign is a long one, there is a danger that routine, boredom and stagnation will ultimately destroy the relationship. A child born under our 6th sign needs particularly careful handling as they can feel fear or embarrassment when communicating with us. Their health often needs increased attention and we should also remember that they are very different from us emotionally.

Finally, we turn to relations with **our own sign**. Scorpio with Scorpio and Cancer with Cancer get along well, but in most other cases, however, our own sign is of little interest to us as it has a similar energy. Sometimes, this relationship can develop as a rivalry, either in business or in love.

There is another interesting detail - we are often attracted to one particular sign. For example, a man's wife and mistress often have the same sign. If there is confrontation between the two, the stronger character displaces the weaker one. As an example, Prince Charles is a Scorpio, while both Princess Diana and Camilla Parker Bowles were born under the sign of Cancer. Camilla was the more assertive and became dominant.

Of course, in order to draw any definitive conclusions, we need an individually prepared horoscope, but the above always, one way or another, manifests itself.

Love description of Zodiac Signs

We know that human sexual behavior has been studied at length. Entire libraries have been written about it, with the aim of helping us understand ourselves and our partners. But is that even possible? It may not be; no matter how smart we are, when it comes to love and sex, there is always an infinite amount to learn. But we have to strive for perfection, and astrology, with its millennia of research, twelve astrological types, and twelve zodiac signs, may hold the key. Below, you will find a brief and accurate description of each zodiac sign's characteristics in love, for both men and women.

Men

ARIES

Aries men are not particularly deep or wise, but they make up for it in sincerity and loyalty. They are active, even aggressive lovers, but a hopeless romantic may be lurking just below the surface. Aries are often monogamous and chivalrous men, for whom there is only one woman (of course, in her absence, they can sleep around with no remorse). If the object of your affection is an Aries, be sure to give him a lot of sex, and remember that for an Aries, when it comes to sex, anything goes. Aries cannot stand women who are negative or disheveled. They need someone energetic, lively, and to feel exciting feelings of romance.

The best partner for an Aries is Cancer, Sagittarius, or Leo. Aquarius can also be a good match, but the relationship will be rather friendly in nature. Partnering with a Scorpio or Taurus will be difficult, but they can be stimulating lovers for an Aries. Virgos are good business contacts, but a poor match as lovers or spouses.

TAURUS

A typical Taurean man is warm, friendly, gentle, and passionate, even if he doesn't always show it. He is utterly captivated by the beauty of the female body, and can find inspiration in any woman. A Taurus has such excess physical and sexual prowess, that to him, sex is a way to relax and calm down. He is the most passionate and emotional lover of the Zodiac, but he expects his partner to take the initiative, and if she doesn't, he will easily find someone else. Taureans rarely divorce, and are true to the end – if not sexually, at least spiritually. They are secretive, keep their cards close, and may have secret lovers. If a Taurus does not feel a deep emotional connection with someone, he won't be shy to ask her friends for their number. He prefers a voluptuous figure over an athletic or skinny woman.

The best partners for a Taurus are Cancer, Virgo, Pisces, or Scorpio. Sagittarius can show a Taurus real delights in both body and spirit, but they are unlikely to make it down the aisle. They can have an interesting relationship with an Aquarius – these signs are very different, but sometimes can spend their lives together. They might initially feel attracted to an Aries, before rejecting her.

GEMINI

The typical Gemini man is easygoing and polite. He is calm, collected, and analytical. For a Gemini, passion is closely linked to intellect, to the point that they will try to find an explanation for their actions before carrying them out. But passion cannot be explained, which scares a Gemini, and they begin jumping from one extreme to the other. This is why you will find more bigamists among Geminis than any other sign of the Zodiac. Sometimes, Gemini men even have two families, or divorce and marry several times throughout the course of their lives. This may be because they simply can't let new and interesting experiences pass them by. A Gemini's wife or lover needs to be smart, quick, and always looking ahead. If she isn't, he will find a new object for his affection.

Aquarians, Libras, and Aries make good partners for a Gemini. A Sagittarius can be fascinating for him, but they will not marry before he reaches middle age, as both partners will be fickle while they are younger. A Gemini and Scorpio are likely to be a difficult match, and the Gemini will try to wriggle out of the Scorpio's tight embrace. A Taurus will be an exciting sex partner, but their partnership won't be for long, and the Taurus is often at fault.

CANCER

Cancers tend to be deep, emotional individuals, who are both sensitive and highly sexual. Their charm is almost mystical, and they know how to use it. Cancers may be the most promiscuous sign of the Zodiac, and open to absolutely anything in bed. Younger Cancers look for women who are more mature, as they are skilled lovers. As they age, they look for someone young enough to be their own daughter, and delight in taking on the role of a teacher. Cancers are devoted to building a family and an inviting home, but once they achieve that goal, they are likely to have a wandering eye. They will not seek moral justification, as they sincerely believe it is simply something everyone does. Their charm works in such a way that women are deeply convinced they are the most important love in a Cancer's life, and that circumstances are the only thing preventing them from being together. Remember that a Cancer man is a master manipulator, and will not be yours unless he is sure you have throngs of admirers. He loves feminine curves, and is turned on by exquisite fragrances. Cancers don't end things with old lovers, and often go back for a visit after a breakup. Another type of Cancer is rarer – a faithful friend, and up for anything in order to provide for his wife and children. He is patriotic and a responsible worker.

Scorpios, Pisces, and other Cancers are a good match. A Taurus can make for a lasting relationship, as both signs place great value on family and are able to get along with one another. A Sagittarius will result in fights and blowouts from the very beginning, followed by conflicts and breakups. The Sagittarius will suffer the most. Marriage to an Aries isn't off the table, but it won't last very long.

LEO

A typical Leo is handsome, proud, and vain, with a need to be the center of attention at all times. They often pretend to be virtuous, until they are able to actually master it. They crave flattery, and prefer women who comply and cater to them. Leos demand unconditional obedience, and constant approval. When a Leo is in love, he is fairly sexual, and capable of being devoted and faithful. Cheap love affairs are not his thing, and Leos are highly aware of how expensive it is to divorce. They make excellent fathers. A Leo's partner needs to look polished and well-dressed, and he will not tolerate either frumpiness or nerds.

Aries, Sagittarius, and Gemini make for good matches. Leos are often very beguiling to Libras; this is the most infamous astrological "master-slave" pairing. Leos are also inexplicably drawn to Pisces – this is the only sign capable of taming them. A Leo and Virgo will face a host of problems sooner or later, and they might be material in nature. The Virgo will attempt to conquer him, and if she does, a breakup is inevitable.

VIRGO

Virgo is a highly intellectual sign, who likes to take a step back and spend his time studying the big picture. But love inherently does not lend itself to analysis, and this can leave Virgos feeling perplexed. While Virgo is taking his time, studying the object of his affection, someone else will swoop in and take her away, leaving him bitterly disappointed. Perhaps for that reason, Virgos tend to marry late, but once they are married, they remain true, and hardly ever initiate divorce. In bed, they are modest and reserved, as they see sex as some sort of quirk of nature, designed solely for procreation. Most Virgos have a gifted sense of taste, hearing, and smell. They cannot tolerate pungent odors and can be squeamish; they believe their partners should always take pains to be very clean. Virgos usually hate over-the-top expressions of love, and are immune to sex as a mean s of control. Many Virgos are stingy and more appropriate as husbands than lovers. Male Virgos tend to be monogamous, though if they are unhappy or disappointed with their partner, they may begin to look for comfort elsewhere and often give in to drunkenness.

Taurus, Capricorn, and Scorpio make the best partners for a Virgo. They may feel inexplicable attraction for Aquarians. They will form friendships with Aries, but rarely will this couple make it down the aisle. With Leos, be careful – this sign is best as a lover, not a spouse.

LIBRA

Libra is a very complex, wishy-washy sign. They are constantly seeking perfection, which often leaves them in discord with the reality around them. Libra men are elegant and refined, and expect no less from their partner. Many Libras treat their partners like a beautiful work of art, and have trouble holding onto the object of their affection. They view love itself as a very abstract concept, and can get tired of the physical aspect of their relationship. They are much more drawn to intrigue and the chase- dreams, candlelit evenings, and other symbols of romance. A high percentage of Libra men are gay, and they view sex with other men as the more elite option. Even when Libras are unhappy in their marriages, they never divorce willingly. Their wives might leave them, however, or they might be taken away by a more decisive partner.

Aquarius and Gemini make the best matches for Libras. Libra can also easily control an independent Sagittarius, and can easily fall under the influence of a powerful and determined Leo, before putting all his strength and effort into breaking free. Relationships with Scorpios are difficult; they may become lovers, but will rarely marry.

SCORPIO

Though it is common to perceive Scorpios as incredibly sexual, they are, in fact, very unassuming, and never brag about their exploits. They will, however, be faithful and devoted to the right woman. The Scorpio man is taciturn, and you can't expect any tender words from him, but he will defend those he loves to the very end. Despite his outward control, Scorpio is very emotional; he needs and craves love, and is willing to fight for it. Scorpios are incredible lovers, and rather than leaving them tired, sex leaves them feeling energized. They are always sexy, even if they aren't particularly handsome. They are unconcerned with the ceremony of wooing you, and more focused on the act of love itself.

Expressive Cancers and gentle, amenable Pisces make the best partners. A Scorpio might also fall under the spell of a Virgo, who is adept at taking the lead. Sparks might fly between two Scorpios, or with a Taurus, who is perfect for a Scorpio in bed. Relationships with Libras, Sagittarians, and Aries are difficult.

SAGITTARIUS

Sagittarian men are lucky, curious, and gregarious. Younger Sagittarians are romantic, passionate, and burning with desire to experience every type of love. Sagittarius is a very idealistic sign, and in that search for perfection, they tend to flit from one partner to another, eventually forgetting what they were even looking for in the first place. A negative Sagittarius might have two or three relationships going on at once, assigning each partner a different day of the week. On the other hand, a positive Sagittarius will channel his powerful sexual energy into creativity, and take his career to new heights. Generally speaking, after multiple relationships and divorces, the Sagittarian man will conclude that his ideal marriage is one where his partner is willing to look the other way.

Aries and Leo make the best matches for a Sagittarius. He might fall under the spell of a Cancer, but would not be happy being married to her. Gemini can be very intriguing, but will only make for a happy marriage after middle age, when both partners are older and wiser. Younger Sagittarians often marry Aquarian women, but things quickly fall apart. Scorpios can make for an interesting relationship, but if the Sagittarius fails to comply, divorce is inevitable.

CAPRICORN

Practical, reserved Capricorn is one of the least sexual signs of the Zodiac. He views sex as an idle way to pass the time, and something he can live without, until he wants to start a family. He tends to marry late, and almost never divorces. Young Capricorns are prone to suppressing their sexual desires, and only discover them later in life, when they have already achieved everything a real man needs – a career and money. We'll be frank – Capricorn is not the best lover, but he can compensate by being caring, attentive, and showering you with valuable gifts. Ever cautious, Capricorn loves to schedule his sexual relationships, and this is something partners will just have to accept. Women should understand that Capricorn needs some help relaxing – perhaps with alcohol. They prefer inconspicuous, unassuming women, and run away from a fashion plate.

The best partners for a Capricorn are Virgo, Taurus, or Scorpio. Cancers might catch his attention, and if they marry, it is likely to be for life. Capricorn is able to easily dominate Pisces, and Pisces-Capricorn is a well-known "slave and master" combination. Relationships with Leos tend to be erratic, and they are unlikely to wed. Aries might make for a cozy family at first, but things will cool off quickly, and often, the marriage only lasts as long as Capricorn is unwilling to make a change in his life.

AQUARIUS

Aquarian men are mercurial, and often come off as peculiar, unusual, or aloof, and detached. Aquarians are turned on by anything novel or strange, and they are constantly looking for new and interesting people. They are stimulated by having a variety of sexual partners, but they consider this to simply be normal life, rather than sexually immoral. Aquarians are unique – they are more abstract than realistic, and can be cold and incomprehensible, even in close relationships. Once an Aquarius gets married, he will try to remain within the realm of decency, but often fails. An Aquarian's partners need uncommon patience, as nothing they do can restrain him. Occasionally, one might encounter another kind of Aquarius – a responsible, hard worker, and exemplary family man.

The best matches for an Aquarius are female fellow Aquarians, Libras, and Sagittarians. When Aquarius seeks out yet another affair, he is not choosy, and will be happy with anyone.

PISCES

Pisces is the most eccentric sign of the Zodiac. This is reflected in his romantic tendencies and sex life. Pisces men become very dependent on those with whom they have a close relationship. Paradoxically, they are simultaneously crafty and childlike when it comes to playing games, and they are easily deceived. As a double bodied sign, Pisces rarely marry just once, as they are very sexual, easily fall in love, and are constantly seeking their ideal. Pisces are very warm people, who love to take care of others and are inclined toward "slave-master" relationships, in which they are the submissive partner. But after catering to so many lovers, Pisces will remain elusive. They are impossible to figure out ahead of time – today, they might be declaring their love for you, but tomorrow, they may disappear – possibly forever! To a Pisces, love is a fantasy, illusion, and dream, and they might spend their whole lives in pursuit of it. Pisces who are unhappy in love are vulnerable to alcoholism or drug addiction.

Cancer and Scorpio make the best partners for a Pisces. He is also easily dominated by Capricorn and Libra, but in turn will conquer even a queen-like Leo. Often, they are fascinated by Geminis – if they marry, it will last a long time, but likely not forever. Relationships with Aries and Sagittarians are erratic, though initially, things can seem almost perfect.

Women

ARIES

Aries women are leaders. They are decisive, bold, and very protective. An Aries can take initiative and is not afraid to make the first move. Her ideal man is strong, and someone she can admire. But remember, at the slightest whiff of weakness, she will knock him off his pedestal. She does not like dull, whiny men, and thinks that there is always a way out of any situation. If she loves someone, she will be faithful. Aries women are too honest to try leading a double life. They are possessive, jealous, and not only will they not forgive those who are unfaithful, their revenge may be brutal; they know no limits. If you can handle an Aries, don't try to put her in a cage; it is best to give her a long leash. Periodically give her some space – then she will seek you out herself. She is sexual, and believe that anything goes in bed.

Her best partners are a Sagittarius or Leo. A Libra can make a good match after middle age, once both partners have grown wiser and settled down a bit. Gemini and Aquarius are only good partners during the initial phase, when everything is still new, but soon enough, they will lose interest in each other. Scorpios are good matches in bed, but only suitable as lovers.

TAURUS

Taurean women possess qualities that men often dream about, but rarely find in the flesh – they are soft, charming, practical, and reliable – they are very caring and will support their partner in every way. A Taurus is highly sexual, affectionate, and can show a man how to take pleasure to new heights. She is also strong and intense. If she is in love, she will be faithful. But when love fades away, she might find someone else on the side, though she will still fight to save her marriage, particularly if her husband earns good money. A Taurus will not tolerate a man who is disheveled or disorganized, and anyone dating her needs to always be on his toes. She will expect gifts, and likes being taken to expensive restaurants, concerts, and other events. If you argue, try to make the first peace offering, because a Taurus finds it very hard to do so – she might withdraw and ruminate for a long time. Never air your dirty laundry; solve all your problems one-on-one.

Scorpio, Virgo, Capricorn, and Cancer make the best matches. A relationship with an Aries or Sagittarius would be difficult. There is little attraction between a Taurus and a Leo, and initially Libras can make for a good partner in bed, but things will quickly cool off and fall apart. A Taurus and Aquarius make an interesting match – despite the difference in signs, their relationships are often lasting, and almost lifelong.

GEMINI

Gemini women are social butterflies, outgoing, and they easily make friends, and then break off the friendship, if people do not hold their interest. A Gemini falls in love hard, is very creative, and often fantasizes about the object of her affection. She is uninterested in sex without any attachment, loves to flirt, and, for the most part, is not particularly affectionate. She dreams of a partner who is her friend, lover, and a romantic, all at once. A Gemini has no use for a man who brings nothing to the table intellectually. That is a tall order, so Geminis often divorce and marry several times. Others simply marry later in life. Once you have begun a life together, do not try to keep her inside – she needs to travel, explore, socialize, attend events and go to the theater. She cannot tolerate possessive men, so avoid giving her the third degree, and remember that despite her flirtatious and social nature, she is, in fact, faithful – as long as you keep her interested and she is in love. Astrologers believe that Geminis do not know what they need until age 29 or 30, so it is best to hold off on marriage until then.

Leo and Libra make the best matches. A relationship with a Cancer is likely, though complex, and depends solely on the Cancer's affection. A Gemini and Sagittarius can have an interesting, dynamic relationship, but these are two restless signs, which might only manage to get together after ages 40-45, once they have had enough thrills out of life and learned to be patient. Relationships with a Capricorn are very difficult, and almost never happen. The honeymoon stage can be wonderful with a Scorpio, but each partner will eventually go their own way, before ending things. A Gemini and Pisces union can also be very interesting – they are drawn to each other, and can have a wonderful relationship, but after a while, the cracks start to show and things will fall apart. An Aquarius is also not a bad match, but they will have little sexual chemistry.

CANCER

Cancers can be divided into two opposing groups. The first includes a sweet and gentle creature who is willing to dedicate her life to her husband and children. She is endlessly devoted to her husband, especially if he makes a decent living and remains faithful. She views all men as potential husbands, which means it is dangerous to strike up a relationship with her if your intentions are not serious; she can be anxious and clingy, sensitive and prone to crying. It is better to break things to her gently, rather than directly spitting out the cold, hard truth. She wants a man who can be a provider, though she often earns well herself. She puts money away for a rainy day, and knows how to be thrifty, for the sake of others around her, rather than only for herself. She is an excellent cook and capable of building an inviting home for her loved ones. She is enthusiastic in bed, a wonderful wife, and a caring mother.

The second type of Cancer is neurotic, and capable of creating a living hell for those around her. She believes that the world is her enemy, and manages to constantly find new intrigue and machinations.

Another Cancer, Virgo, Taurus, Scorpio, and Pisces make the best matches. A Cancer can often fall in love with a Gemini, but eventually, things will grow complicated, as she will be exhausted by a Gemini's constant mood swings and cheating. A Cancer and Sagittarius will initially have passionate sex, but things will quickly cool off. A relationship with a Capricorn is a real possibility, but only later in life, as while they are young, they are likely to fight and argue constantly. Cancer can also have a relationship with an Aries, but this will not be easy.

LEO

Leos are usually beautiful or charming, and outwardly sexual. And yet, appearances can be deceiving – they are not actually that interested in sex. Leo women want to be the center of attention and men running after them boosts their self-esteem, but they are more interested in their career, creating something new, and success than sex. They often have high-powered careers and are proud of their own achievements. Their partners need to be strong; if a Leo feels a man is weak, she can carry him herself for a while- before leaving him. It is difficult for her to find a partner for life, as chivalrous knights are a dying breed, and she is not willing to compromise. If you are interested in a Leo, take the initiative, admire her, and remember that even a queen is still a woman. Timid men or tightwads need not apply. Leos like to help others, but they don't need a walking disaster in their life. If they are married and in love, they are usually faithful, and petty gossip isn't their thing. Leo women make excellent mothers, and are ready to give their lives to their children. Their negative traits include vanity and a willingness to lie, in order to make themselves look better.

Sagittarius, Aries, and Libra make the best matches. Leos can also have an interesting relationship with a Virgo, though both partners will weaken each other. Life with a Taurus will lead to endless arguments – both signs are very stubborn, and unwilling to give in. Leos and Pisces are another difficult pair, as she will have to learn to be submissive if she wants to keep him around. A relationship with a Capricorn will work if there is a common denominator, but they will have little sexual chemistry. Life with a Scorpio will be turbulent to say the least, and they will usually break up later in life.

VIRGO

Virgo women are practical, clever, and often duplicitous. Marrying one isn't for everyone. She is a neat freak to the point of annoying those around her. She is also an excellent cook, and strives to ensure her children receive the very best by teaching them everything, and preparing them for a bright future. She is also thrifty – she won't throw money around, and, in fact, won't even give it to her husband. She has no time for rude, macho strongmen, and is suspicious of spendthrifts. She will not be offended if you take her to a cozy and modest café rather than an elegant restaurant. Virgos are masters of intrigue, and manage to outperform every other sign of the Zodiac in this regard. Virgos love to criticize everyone and everything; to listen to them, the entire world is simply a disaster and wrong, and only she is the exception to this rule. Virgos are not believed to be particularly sexual, but there are different variations when it comes to this. Rarely, one finds an open-minded Virgo willing to try anything, and who does it all on a grand scale – but she is rather the exception to this general rule.

The best matches for a Virgo are Cancer, Taurus, and Capricorn. She also can get along well with a Scorpio, but will find conflict with Sagittarius. A Pisces will strike her interest, but they will rarely make it down the aisle. She is often attracted to an Aquarius, but they would drive each other up the wall were they to actually marry. An Aries forces Virgo to see another side of life, but here, she will have to learn to conform and adapt.

LIBRA

Female Libras tend to be beautiful, glamorous, or very charming. They are practical, tactical, rational, though they are adept at hiding these qualities behind their romantic and elegant appearance. Libras are drawn to marriage, and are good at imagining the kind of partner they need. They seek out strong, well-off men and are often more interested in someone's social status and bank account than feelings. The object of their affection needs to be dashing, and have a good reputation in society. Libras love expensive things, jewelry, and finery. If they are feeling down, a beautiful gift will instantly cheer them up. They will not tolerate scandal or conflict, and will spend all their energy trying to keep the peace, or at least the appearance thereof. They do not like to air their dirty laundry, and will only divorce in extreme circumstances. They are always convinced they are right and react to any objections as though they have been insulted. Most Libras are not particularly sexual, except those with Venus or the Moon in Scorpio.

Leos, Geminis, and Aquarians make good matches. Libra women are highly attracted to Aries men - this is a real case of opposites attract. They can get along with a Sagittarius, though he will find that Libras are too proper and calm. Capricorn, Pisces, and Cancer are all difficult matches. Things will begin tumultuously with a Taurus, before each partner goes his or her own way.

SCORPIO

Scorpio women may appear outwardly restrained, but there is much more bubbling below the surface. They are ambitious with high self-esteem, but often wear a mask of unpretentiousness. They are the true power behind the scenes, the one who holds the family together, but never talk about it. Scorpios are strong-willed, resilient, and natural survivors. Often, Scorpios are brutally honest, and expect the same out of those around them. They do not like having to conform, and attempt to get others to adapt to them, as they honestly believe everyone will be better off that way. They are incredibly intuitive, and not easily deceived. They have an excellent memory, and can quickly figure out which of your buttons to push. They are passionate in bed, and their temperament will not diminish with age. When she is sexually frustrated, a Scorpio will throw all of her energy into her career or her loved ones. She is proud, categorical, and "if you don't do it right, don't do it at all" is her motto. Scorpio cannot be fooled, and she will not forgive any cheating. Will she cheat herself? Yes! But it will not break up her family, and she will attempt to keep it a secret. Scorpios are usually attractive to men, even if they are not particularly beautiful. They keep a low profile, though they always figure out their partner, and give them some invisible sign. There is also another, selfish type of Scorpio, who will use others for as long as they need them, before unceremoniously casting them aside.

Taurus is a good match; they will have excellent sexual chemistry and understand each other. Scorpio and Gemini are drawn to each other, but are unlikely to stay together long enough to actually get married. Cancer can be a good partner as well, but Cancers are possessive, while Scorpios do not like others meddling in their affairs, though they can later resolve their arguments in bed. Scorpio and Leo are often found together, but their relationship can also be very complicated. Leos are animated and chipper, while Scorpios, who are much deeper and more stubborn, see Leos as not particularly serious or reliable. One good example of this is Bill (a Leo) and Hillary (a Scorpio) Clinton. Virgo can also make a good partner, but when Scorpio seemingly lacks emotions, he will look for them elsewhere. Relationships with Lira are strange and very rare. Scorpio sees Libra as too insecure, and Libra does not appreciate Scorpio's rigidity. Two Scorpios together make an excellent marriage! Sagittarius and Scorpio are unlikely to get together, as she will think he is shallow and rude. If they do manage to get married, Scorpio's drive and persistence is the only thing that will make the marriage last. Capricorn is also not a bad match, and while Scorpio finds Aquarius attractive, they will rarely get married, as they are simply speaking different languages! Things are alright with a Pisces, as both signs are emotional, and Pisces can let Scorpio take the lead when necessary.

SAGITTARIUS

Sagittarius women are usually charming, bubbly, energetic, and have the gift of gab. They are kind, sincere, and love people. They are also straightforward, fair, and very ambitious, occasionally to the point of irritating those around them. But telling them something is easier than not telling them, and they often manage to win over their enemies. Sagittarius tends to have excellent intuition, and she loves to both learn and teach others. She is a natural leader, and loves taking charge at work and at home. Many Sagittarian women have itchy feet, and prefer all kinds of travel to sitting at home. They are not particularly good housewives – to be frank, cooking and cleaning is simply not for them. Their loved ones must learn to adapt to them, but Sagittarians themselves hate any pressure. They are not easy for men to handle, as Sagittarians want to be in charge. Sagittarius falls in love easily, is very sexual and temperamental, and may marry multiple times. Despite outward appearances, Sagittarius is a very lonely sign. Even after she is married with children, she may continue living as if she were alone; you might say she marches to the beat of her own drum. Younger

Sagittarians can be reckless, but as they mature, they can be drawn to religion, philosophy, and the occult.

Aries and Leo make the best matches, as Sagittarius is able to bend to Leo's ways, or at least pretend to. Sagittarians often end up with Aquarians, but their marriages do not tend to be for the long haul. They are attracted to Geminis, but are unlikely to marry one until middle age, when both signs have settled down. Sagittarius and Cancer have incredible sexual chemistry, but an actual relationship between them would be tumultuous and difficult. Capricorn can make a good partner- as long as they are able to respect each other's quirks. Sagittarius rarely ends up with a Virgo, and while she may often meet Pisces, things are unlikely to go very far.

CAPRICORN

Capricorn women are conscientious, reliable, organized, and hard-working. Many believe that life means nothing but work, and live accordingly. They are practical, and not particularly drawn to parties or loud groups of people. But if someone useful will be there, they are sure to make an appearance. Capricorn women are stingy, but not as much as their male counterparts. They are critical of others, but think highly of themselves. Generally, they take a difficult path in life, but thanks to their dedication, perseverance, and willingness to push their own limits, they are able to forge their own path, and by 45 or 50, they can provide themselves with anything they could want. Capricorn women have the peculiarity of looking older than their peers when they are young, and younger than everyone else once they have matured. They are not particularly sexual, and tend to be faithful partners. They rarely divorce, and even will fight until the end, even for a failed marriage. Many Capricorns have a pessimistic outlook of life, and have a tendency to be depressed. They are rarely at the center of any social circle, but are excellent organizers. They have a very rigid view of life and love, and are not interested in a fling, as marriage is the end goal. As a wife, Capricorn is simultaneously difficult and reliable. She is difficult because of her strict nature and difficulty adapting. But she will also take on all the household duties, and her husband can relax, knowing his children are in good hands.

Taurus, Pisces, and Scorpio make good matches. Aries is difficult, once things cool off after the initial honeymoon. When a Capricorn meets another Capricorn, they will be each other's first and last love. Sagittarius isn't a bad match, but they don't always pass the test of time. Aquarius and Capricorn are a difficult match, and rarely found together. Things are too dull with a Virgo, and while Leo can be exciting at first, things will fall apart when he begins showing off. Libra and Aquarius are both difficult partners for Capricorn, and she is rarely found with either of them.

AQUARIUS

A female Aquarius is very different from her male counterparts. She is calm and keeps a cool head, but she is also affectionate and open. She values loyalty above all else, and is unlikely to recover from any infidelity, though she will only divorce if this becomes a chronic trend, and she has truly been stabbed in the back. She is not interested in her partner's money, but rather, his professional success. She is unobtrusive and trusting, and will refrain from listening in on her partner's phone conversations or hacking into his email. With rare exceptions, Aquarian women make terrible housewives. But they are excellent partners in life – they are faithful, never boring, and will not reject a man, even in the most difficult circumstances. Most Aquarians are highly intuitive, and can easily tell the truth from a lie. They themselves only lie in extreme situations, which call for a "white lie" in order to avoid hurting someone's feelings.

Aquarius gets along well with Aries, Gemini, and Libra. She can also have a good relationship with a Sagittarius. Taurus often makes a successful match, though they are emotionally very different; the same goes for Virgo. Aquarius and Scorpio, Capricorn, or Cancer is a difficult match. Pisces can make a good partner as well, as both signs complement each other. Any relationship with a Leo will be tumultuous, but lasting, as Leo is selfish, and Aquarius will therefore have to be very forgiving.

PISCES

Pisces women are very adaptable, musically inclined, and erotic. They possess an innate earthly wisdom, and a good business sense. Pisces often reinvent themselves; they can be emotional, soft, and obstinate, as well as sentimental, at times. Their behavioral changes can be explained by frequent ups and downs. Pisces is charming, caring, and her outward malleability is very attractive to men. She is capable of loving selflessly, as long as the man has something to love. Even if he doesn't, she will try and take care of him until the very end. Pisces' greatest fear is poverty. They are intuitive, vulnerable, and always try to avoid conflict. They love to embellish the truth, and sometimes alcohol helps with this. Rarely, one finds extremely unbalanced, neurotic and dishonest Pisces, who are capable of turning their loved ones' lives into a living Hell!

Taurus, Capricorn, Cancer, and Scorpio make the best matches. She will be greatly attracted to a Virgo, but a lasting relationship is only likely if both partners are highly spiritual. Any union with a Libra is likely to be difficult and full of conflict. Pisces finds Gemini attractive, and they may have a very lively relationship – for a while. Occasionally, Pisces ends up with a Sagittarius, but she will have to fade into the background and entirely submit to him. If she ends up with an Aquarius, expect strong emotional outbursts, and a marriage that revolves around the need to raise their children.

Tatiana Borsch

Printed in Great Britain
by Amazon

51646869R00040